PRACTICAL LANGUAGE TEACHING

Editors: Marion Geddes and Gill Sturtridge

No. 2

Using the Magnetboard

PRACTICAL LANGUAGE TEACHING
Editors: Marion Geddes and Gill Sturtridge

Using the Magnetboard

DONN BYRNE

London
GEORGE ALLEN & UNWIN
Boston   Sydney

First published in 1980

GEORGE ALLEN & UNWIN LTD
40 Museum Street, London WC1A 1LU

© George Allen & Unwin (Publishers) Ltd, 1980

British Library Cataloguing in Publication Data

Byrne, Donn, *b. 1929*
  Using the magnetboard.—(Practical
language teaching; no. 2).
1. Language and languages—Study and
teaching—Audio-visual aids
2. Magnetic boards
I. Title II. Series
418'.007'8   P53   79-40018

ISBN 0-04-371065-4

Typeset in 10 on 12 point Times by Trade Linotype Ltd, Birmingham
and printed in Great Britain
by Hazell Watson & Viney Ltd, Aylesbury

Contents

Acknowledgements

Some of the ideas in this book were first published in my article 'Making and Using the Magnetboard' which has appeared in the following journals
Lingua e Nuova Didattica vol. 1, no. 1 (1972)
English Teaching Forum vol. XII, no. 2 (1974)
Modern English Teacher vol. 5, no. 1 (1977)
Figs. 20 and 21 are reproduced from *Progressive Picture Compositions,* Donn Byrne © Longman Group Ltd (1967)
Particular thanks are due to Susan Holden for the photographic illustrations

1 *Introduction*

This book sets out to provide a comprehensive guide to the magnetboard. It deals with the magnetboard itself and with the materials you will need for it, and shows you how you can make these for yourself. It also describes and illustrates the various uses of the magnetboard in the classroom as an aid to developing language skills (listening, speaking, reading and writing). It is hoped that the guidance this book offers will encourage you to make greater use of the magnetboard in your teaching.

Since this book deals exclusively with the magnetboard and refers to other aids only for the purpose of comparison, it is inevitable that to some extent it will appear to give this aid undue importance in language teaching. After you have read about the numerous and varied uses that the magnetboard can be put to, you may conclude that you could do without many other aids. This would be wrong. Viewed in perspective, it is only one of a range of aids which you must evaluate and relate to your teaching situation. If you look at the magnetboard in this light, you will then be able to make the most effective and appropriate use of it in *your* classroom.

2 *The Magnetboard and Its Materials*

This chapter deals with the magnetboard and the various materials which you need to go with it. Although many of these are available commercially, it is quite easy to make them for yourself. Detailed guidance is given below on how to do this.

2.1 THE MAGNETBOARD

If you work in a school or institute with up-to-date equipment, it is possible that your blackboard (or whiteboard) is magnetic. Provided that your board is big enough for you to display material and write on it at the same time, you will not need to acquire or make a magnetboard like the one described below.

In its simplest form, the magnetboard is a sheet of metal which has been mounted on a sheet of wood, such as plywood or hardboard, or framed so that the sharp edges of the metal are covered. The metal itself is not in fact magnetic but it must be of the kind that attracts magnetic material. Two metals commonly used are zinc or tin plate. Even tin cans can be opened up and flattened to provide a surface for a magnetboard! Alloys are not suitable.

If the magnetboard does not have to be carried from one classroom to another but can be attached to the wall (e.g. at the side of the blackboard), an ideal size is about 1 square metre. Usually, however, equipment has to be shared by several teachers—or perhaps you would like to have a board of your own. In this case the ideal size for a portable magnetboard is about 70 cm by 50 cm (2 ft by 1 ft 6 in). This enables you to carry it comfortably under your arm.

Figure 1 shows the reverse side of a portable folding magnetboard. It is quite easy to make.

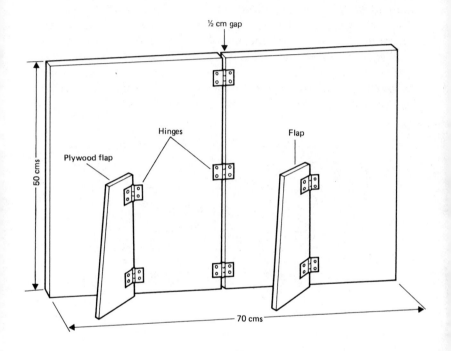

Figure 1

You need two sheets of metal and two sheets of wood, each 35 cm by 50 cm. The sheets of metal may be glued or screwed to the wood. Two additional pieces of wood, as shown in the diagram, serve as flaps. The flaps open out at right angles to the board to support it in an upright position on a table. Be careful to attach the flaps to the left-hand side of each section of the board so that they are not in contact when the board is folded.

2.1.1   USE OF THE MAGNETBOARD

The magnetboard is a useful device for the display of any visual material: wall pictures, charts, magazine cutouts, photos, cards for teaching reading, and so on. Wall pictures and other large charts are best kept in position by placing magnetic counters (see 2.3) in each corner, as shown in Figure 2. The advantages of using a magnetboard for this purpose are (*a*) it is easy to put material in position on the board and to move it around or replace it with new material and (*b*) it stays securely in position.

Our more specific concern, however, is with the use of the magnetboard in conjunction with specially designed materials: backdrops and cutouts. These are described below.

Figure 2

2.2   BACKDROPS

A backdrop is like a very simple piece of stage scenery. It is a large sheet of thin white paper which you attach to the magnetboard by placing a magnetic counter in each corner, as shown in Figure 3.

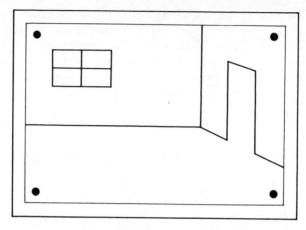

Figure 3

On a practical level, backdrops provide a uniform colour for your magnetboard (which, if it is commercially produced, may be green or grey). It ensures that your cutouts stand out against the white background and also that the white edges of the cutouts will not show up (on the importance of not cutting too closely round the edges of cutouts, see 2.3.1).

Figure 4

Pedagogically, the backdrop helps to contextualise language practice. Although you can use a magnetboard without using backdrops, as shown in Figure 4, the material lacks a setting, which will in most cases make the language work you do with it less interesting, less realistic and therefore less memorable for the learners. Compare the same material in the context of a backdrop (Figure 5).

The difference should be immediately apparent.

Figure 5

2.2.1 MAKING BACKDROPS

The first thing to notice about backdrops is that they are extremely simple: no more than an outline, in fact, boldly drawn, with just enough detail to convey the setting. By keeping the detail to a minimum, you can use the same backdrop for different scenes. Thus, by the use of appropriate cutouts, you can convert your sitting-room, as shown in 2.2 above, into a bedroom or a kitchen (Figures 6 and 7). It is the simplicity of the backdrop that makes it multi-purpose.

You should decide in the light of your own teaching situation what kind of backdrops you will need. However, you might begin by making some general basic backdrops which are likely

Figures 6 and 7

to be of use in many teaching situations. You can then add others to meet your specific requirements. For example, if you are teaching commercial English, you may want to have a backdrop of a room which looks more precisely like an office. Some general basic backdrops are illustrated in Figures 8, 9 and 10.

Figure 8

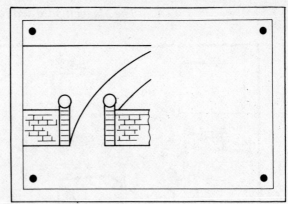

Figure 9

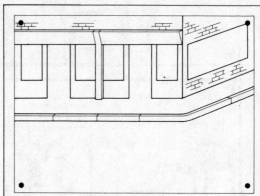

Figure 10

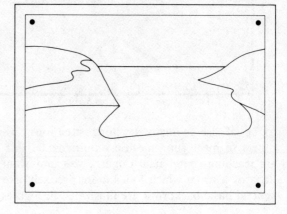

~hould always use thin sheets of paper.
~ps are dispensable. A more important
~at thick paper will not stay in place on the
~ also reduces the amount of magnetic contact
~uts and the magnetboard. This matters a great
~ place one cutout on top of another.

CUTOUTS

This term is used to describe different kinds of visual material
which are superimposed on the backdrops. A cutout is held in
place on the board either by putting a magnetic counter over it
(as shown in 2.1.1) or by attaching one or more pieces of
magnetic strip (depending on the size of the cutout) to the
reverse side, as shown in Figure 11.

Figure 11

We have already seen how the same backdrop can be used to
represent different rooms by changing the cutouts. In Figure 12
you can see how the same cutouts can be manipulated to produce
a different version of the room scene in Figure 5. It is the use of
cutouts that makes the magnetboard an extremely flexible and

Figure 12

economical teaching device. With just a single backdrop and a few cutouts you can create many different scenes quickly and easily. You can also create unusual—and for the learners memorable—ones, as shown in Figure 13.

Figure 13

2.3.1 MAKING CUTOUTS

You should use a good-quality stiff card (either matt or glossy) for making cutouts, because they have to stand up to a good deal of handling both by you and by the students. The only other essential equipment is a set of felt-tipped pens of different colours or crayons. Paints may also be used. White ink is useful for erasing mistakes.

After you have sketched an object in pencil, give it a bold outline in black and then colour appropriately. Do not put in too much detail and do not worry too much about the quality of your drawings. Cutouts that seem crude when viewed from close up are perfectly acceptable—and often more visible—when seen from a distance, which is how your students will see them. If you want to draw, for example, a house and you feel unsure of your ability to do this adequately, copy or trace a suitable picture from a book or magazine. You may even find a certain amount of ready-made material in magazines (e.g. cars) but in the long run you will find it quicker and more satisfying to learn to make your own.

Figure 14

When drawing people, you can use either stick figures or more substantial figures, as illustrated in Figure 14. Remember that people as well as other objects such as chairs and cars should be shown facing in different directions (Figure 15).

Figure 15

Do not worry too much about proportion. It is inevitable that a small object such as a bottle must be drawn out of proportion to a table, otherwise it would not be visible from the back of the classroom (see Figure 16). Also, very small objects are not easy to handle. In fact, the lack of proportion matters less because

Figure 16

objects have no *permanent* relationship with one another (as they do in a picture).

An important point to keep in mind when making cutouts is to leave a broad cutting edge where necessary. This will not show up on the white backdrop. If you try to cut too carefully round the edges of your cutout, this not only adds to your work but may also weaken the cutout at certain points (e.g. the legs of a TV set). See Figure 17.

Figure 17

It was mentioned in 2.3 that you may use either counters or strip to attach your cutouts to the magnetboard. If you simply place a counter on top of the cutout, obviously you will need far less magnetic material (eighteen counters is about what you will require). On the other hand, magnetic strip (or small magnets) permanently attached to the reverse side of the cutouts will make it easier for you to handle the material and also allow one cutout to be superimposed on another (see Figure 50).

2.3.2 SUGGESTIONS FOR A BASIC SET OF CUTOUTS

The lists below are intended only to indicate the lines along which you can develop your basic set of general-purpose cutouts. You will need to expand these and also to add items that relate specifically to your classroom requirements. In particular, you will probably want to include 'characters' from your textbook.

(a) *People* (Figures 18 and 19)

adults: working, carrying something, talking, reading, dancing (etc.)

children: running, jumping, playing (ball), watching (TV) (etc.)

occupations (men and women): shop assistants, a doctor, a postman, a policeman (etc.)

Make sure that you incorporate differences relating to age, size (tall/short, fat/thin), general appearance (long/short hair, with or without glasses, etc.) and clothes.

Figure 18

Figure 19

(b) *Objects found in or around the house* (Figures 20, 21 and 22)
furniture: tables, chairs, armchairs, beds, a bookcase (etc.)

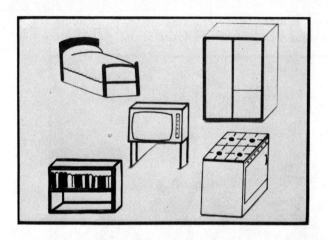

Figure 20

Notice that you can draw either two- or three-dimensional objects, as shown. The three-dimensional table gives, of course, a broader surface to place other objects on.

For furniture do not use full colour: it is sufficient just to colour the edges (e.g. brown). If most of the piece of furniture (e.g. a table) is left white, this helps any object placed on or in front of it to stand out clearly.

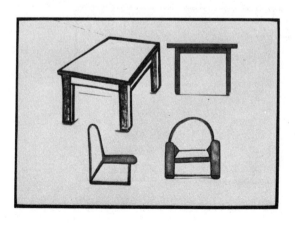

Figure 21

smaller objects: lamps, clocks, pictures, baskets, an umbrella, a vase of flowers, saucepans, items of clothing (etc.)

You should include two of several objects, making them different in some way (e.g. size, colour).

Figure 22

(c) *Objects for the general exterior scene* (see 2.2.1)
trees, animals, a pond, a flowerbed, a bench, clouds, the sun, the moon (etc.)

Figure 23

You may wish to include several different kinds of house which can be used in this context, but you should have one large house which can be 'converted' by means of different signs, as shown in Figure 24.

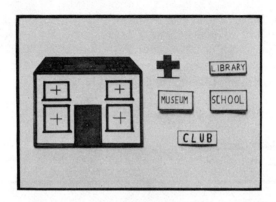

Figure 24

(d) *Objects for the street scene* (Figure 25)
cars, buses, lorries, shop windows, street signs (etc.)

Figure 25

The shop windows enable you to use your backdrop of the street to show different kinds of shops. Shops are probably best represented by a 'symbol' of some kind (e.g. an orange and a banana for a greengrocer's).

(e) *Objects seen on or near the beach*
different kinds of boats (rowing boat, yacht, steamer), a lighthouse, some rocks, a large umbrella, a beachball (etc.); you will also need people dressed for the beach and engaged in activities such as swimming, playing (ball), sunbathing (etc.)

Two other useful items for your basic set of cutouts are:

(i) *Balloons* (Figure 26)
to indicate that people are talking.

Figure 26

(ii) *Figures of people* (Figure 27)
various items of clothing can be superimposed on these for the purpose of discussing what people are wearing, what they might wear and what different clothes they are wearing.

Figure 27

2.4   THE STORAGE OF MAGNETBOARD MATERIALS

Backdrops may be rolled and kept in a cardboard cylinder. Because the paper is thin, they open out easily for use on the magnetboard.

Cutouts may be stored in plastic or paper envelopes or in boxes. If you have attached magnetic material to the reverse side of the cutouts, it is better to use a roomy box so that the cutouts do not get scratched. To protect your cutouts (also against handling) you may cover them with 'transpaseal' or other similar material.

Whatever system you adopt for storing your cutouts:

(a)   group them in *sets*. Label the container and list the contents;
(b)   keep all magnetic material (counters, cutouts with magnetic strip attached) well clear of recorded tapes. The recordings can easily be damaged. You must never carry tapes and magnetic material together in your bag.

2.5 THE MAGNETBOARD COMPARED WITH OTHER AIDS

2.5.1 THE FLANNELGRAPH

The magnetboard has many features in common with the flannel-graph. Both make use of cutouts which can be manipulated to produce contexts for language practice. Unless, however, you have a number of flannelgraphs with outline scenes drawn on them, the use of backdrops on the magnetboard makes it possible to provide a much fuller context for language practice. In general, it is easier to move cutouts around on the magnetboard and there is much less risk of displacing other cutouts when you do so. Another important point in favour of the magnetboard is that it is possible to place cutouts in front of or behind others.

2.5.2 THE OVERHEAD PROJECTOR

It is possible to adapt many of the ideas in the preceding sections (2.2 and 2.3) for use with the overhead projector. For example, you can reproduce a backdrop (e.g. of the room) on a transparency and superimpose small cutouts, also made out of transparent material. These can be manipulated as for the magnetboard.

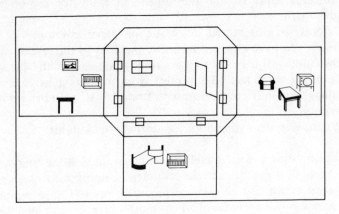

Figure 28

However, because the objects are very small, they are difficult to handle. One way of reducing this difficulty is to provide alternative scenes, with the furniture in different positions, as shown in Figure 28. In this way you have a smaller number of objects to handle but you can still produce many variations of the same scene (see Figure 29).

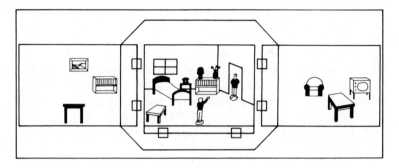

Figure 29

One great advantage of using the overhead projector as an alternative to the magnetboard is that the materials are much less bulky to carry around and to store. The cutouts are also reversible.

2.5.3 WALL PICTURES

Wall pictures have the great disadvantage of being static: the scene never changes. To develop effective language around a wall picture calls for ingenuity on the part of the teacher and co-operation on the part of the students—at least if the picture is to be exploited imaginatively (e.g. for teaching different tenses). On the other hand, if you want, for example, to practise past time with magnetboard materials, the cutouts can actually be taken away, so that you can meaningfully ask: 'Where was the . . .?' (see, for example, Figures 54 and 55). The class may also be *actively involved* in 'building up' a scene on the magnetboard: that is, in suggesting which cutouts might be used and where they might be placed.

It should be clear from the preceding sections that you need only a small amount of magnetboard material to do the work of several wall pictures. On the other hand, it should be acknowledged that attractively produced pictures are likely to have a greater visual appeal for certain learners and of course they are much better suited to certain types of language work (e.g. discussion). They are also much easier to carry around.

2.5.4 THE BLACKBOARD

The magnetboard should not be regarded as an alternative to the blackboard but rather as a way of supplementing it. If you can draw, there will be many occasions when you can use the blackboard for quick sketches which will serve much the same purpose as scenes created on the magnetboard. Clearly, however, the magnetboard has many advantages for the teacher who is not skilled at spontaneous drawing.

If your blackboard (or whiteboard) is magnetic, you can of course draw the equivalent of a backdrop on it and superimpose the cutouts directly. If it is not magnetic, you can still attach cutouts to it by means of 'blutack' or a similar substance. (Blutack is a plastic adhesive, rather like sticky clay.) However, they are not so easy to manipulate as on the magnetboard.

2.6 SOME MAGNETBOARD SCENES

This chapter on materials concludes with some scenes to illustrate the flexibility of the magnetboard.

Figure 30

Figure 31

Figure 32

Figure 33

Figure 34

Figure 35

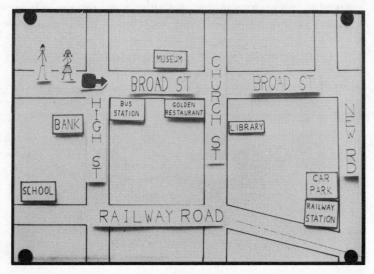

Figure 36

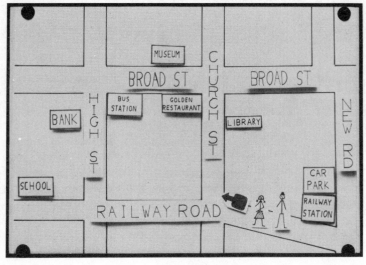

Figure 37

While the students listen, all the objects referred to, except for the briefcase and the camera, which can be left at the side of the magnetboard, are put in position in the room (Figure 39).

The students can then be asked to listen to a second version of the story, with the objects arranged in different positions on the board. As a check on listening comprehension, one or two objects could be put in the wrong place and the students asked to spot the mistakes.

It should be noted that the text could include more advanced language items such as passive forms. *The table had been over-turned ... His books had been thrown on the floor ... His brief-case had been stolen!*

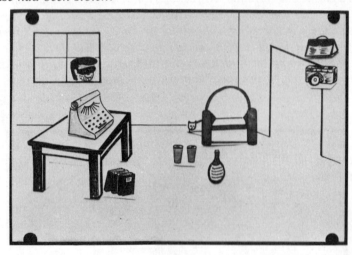

Figure 39

3.2.2 AN EXAMPLE AT AN ADVANCED LEVEL

A talk—for example, a description of a town—may be accompanied by diagrammatic material on the magnetboard. Figure 40 shows the backdrop of a town and the areas into which it is divided. These can be put in position while the students listen to the talk. This setting is further exploited for written work in 3.9.3.

3 *Using the Magnetboard: Techniques and Procedures*

3.1 THE POTENTIAL OF THE MAGNETBOARD AT DIFFERENT STAGES OF LEARNING AND FOR TEACHING DIFFERENT SKILLS

The magnetboard is especially useful for the presentation of new language material and for the creation of a wide range of contexts in which to practise it. However, *someone* has to manipulate the material on the board and consequently the magnetboard has no special value as an aid for pair or group work, and in general is not a very useful aid at the production (or extension) stage of learning.

In terms of skills, it is most useful for teaching oral production, including oral activities that lead on to writing. It has some use as an aid to listening comprehension and for teaching reading and writing in the early stages.

3.1.1 THE IMPORTANCE OF SELECTING MATERIAL

All the activities described in this section depend for their success on the *careful selection* of magnetboard material at the lesson preparation stage. Because the material is easy to manipulate, there is always the temptation to improvise contexts for practice. Although these may be interesting and amusing, they will not however greatly contribute to learning. While preparing your lesson you must therefore consider whether the magnetboard is likely to be the most effective aid for your purpose and, if it is, which materials you will need. Arrange your materials carefully before you go into class and never take in more than you need. Some 'rehearsal' is usually necessary beforehand.

3.2   THE MAGNETBOARD AS AN AID TO LISTENING COMPREHENSION

Some kind of visual accompaniment, pictorial or diagrammatic, to a spoken text is often either an appropriate or a necessary aid to listening. Listening alone, even to well-recorded material, can be an artificial activity without some kind of support. In most situations, for example, we can actually see the speakers while they are talking and watch their facial expressions and gestures. In addition, in more formal listening situations, talks are commonly accompanied by some form of illustration, such as diagrams and outlines, and by key phrases and words on the blackboard.

Clearly any of the aids discussed in 2.5 might be used for this purpose and the magnetboard is examined below principally with a view to identifying its special advantages. There are two to be noted:

(a)   It is possible to put material easily and quickly on the board while the students are listening in order to focus attention on certain points.

(b)   Because the material is flexible, it can be manipulated to produce modified or parallel illustrations of the text which the students have heard. This is a useful way of reinforcing listening material or of checking listening comprehension.

Two examples of using the magnetboard as an aid to listening comprehension are given below in 3.2.1 and 3.2.2. These activities might lead on to related oral or written work. It should also be noted that the procedure for presenting a dialogue in conjunction with magnetboard materials at the end of 3.3 is also a listening comprehension activity.

3.2.1   AN EXAMPLE AT AN ELEMENTARY LEVEL

The students can be asked to listen, either to you or prefer recorded text, while items are located on the magnetboar moment they are referred to. Here, for example, is a sho about a man who arrived home late one night and fou someone had broken into the house. The setting for this magnetboard is shown in Figure 38.

The story runs:

When he came into the sitting-room, he noticed that his books lying on the floor near the table. There was a bottle on the floo and some glasses. He looked for his typewriter. That was sti the table. But where was his briefcase? It wasn't there! His car wasn't there either! And what about his cat? His cat wasn't th either . . . but people don't steal cats, he thought. But then he sa . . . hiding behind the armchair . . . afraid. And then, as he look round the room, he saw something else . . . A face at the window!

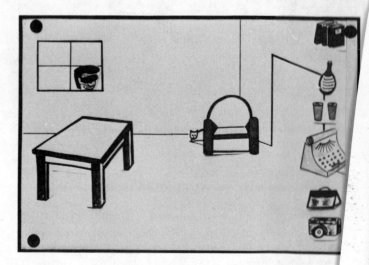

Figure 38

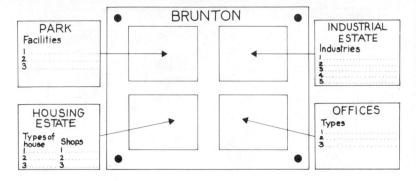

Figure 40

3.3 THE MAGNETBOARD AS AN AID TO PRESENTING A TEXT

Your coursebook is likely to contain many texts (dialogues, stories, descriptions) for which the magnetboard will be useful when you are trying to get across their meaning to the class. It was suggested in 2.3.2 that you might make magnetboard cutouts of characters that appear in your textbook. These can be used in a number of ways. For example, if you do not have a recording of a dialogue and have to read it aloud to the class, you can place these figures on the magnetboard and point to them to show who is speaking. (This is an adaptation of a technique suggested by J. Y. K. Kerr in his article 'Reading a dialogue aloud to a class', *Modern English Teacher*, vol. 5, no. 3.)

You can also use these figures in conjunction with other cues both for presentation and recall. They will be more effective, of course, within the context of a backdrop, as shown in Figure 41. This scene provides a context for a dialogue that begins:

Woman: Have you seen a small girl with a dog?
Man: Yes, near the house over there.
Woman: What was she doing?
Man: Well, I think she was climbing a tree ...

Figure 41

Keywords can also be put in the balloons when you want to cue the dialogue for recall (see Figure 42).

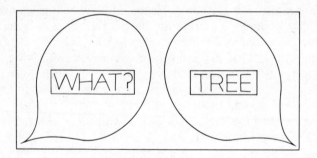

Figure 42

For continuous prose texts such as stories it may be sufficient to place cutouts of key items in sequence on the magnetboard (Figure 43). These cutouts, placed one at a time on the magnetboard, can be used both for presenting the following story and for cueing it at the recall stage.

After breakfast, Mike went to town by bus. He got there at nine o'clock. First of all he went to the bookshop and bought some books. As he was coming out of the bookshop, he met a friend, and they went and had a coffee together.

Figure 43

In the example below, a map is used for presenting a dialogue which is mainly concerned with asking for and giving directions. The dialogue runs as follows:

John has just arrived in town. He rings up his friend Peter, who is at home, from the station. Peter answers the phone.

Peter: 892-7464.
John: Peter, it's me . . . John.
Peter: John! Where are you? At the station?
John: Yes . . .
Peter: Well, come round to the house.

John: How do I get there? By taxi?

Peter: No, you can walk. It's not very far. Listen. Go out of the station and turn left into the High Street.

John: All right.

Peter: Go up the High Street ... past the car park ... and you'll see a bank on the corner. Cross the road and turn right into Broad Street. Cross the road again and turn left into Church Street—there's a museum on the corner. I live about two hundred yards up on the right ...

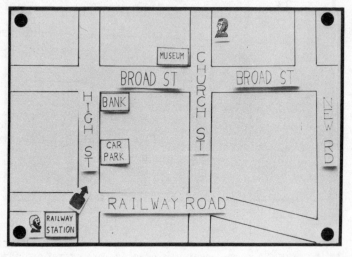

Figure 44

As for the listening comprehension exercise in 3.2.1, the cutouts—in this case the names of the places John will pass on his way to Peter's house—should be placed on the map while the students are listening to the dialogue. A cutout with an arrow on it can also be moved along the route John has to follow (Figure 44).

For further practice in asking for and giving directions, John's starting point (perhaps the bus station) can be located in some other position on the map, together with different places (library, restaurant, school) which he has to pass by. One example is given in

Figure 45 but clearly the setting can be exploited in many other ways.

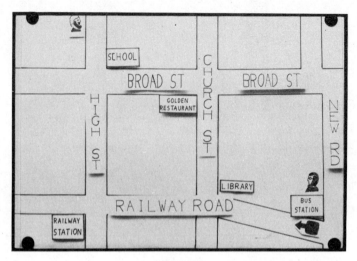

Figure 45

3.3.1 THE MAGNETBOARD AS AN AID TO PRESENTING A TECHNICAL DESCRIPTION

If you are teaching scientific or technical English, you may wish to use the magnetboard to describe, for example, how something works. For this purpose you may superimpose one cutout on top of another to show first the exterior of the object and then the interior, with yet a third cutout if you want to show the object in greater depth. You can also divide the object up into sections. If, for example, you wanted to show how a light bulb worked, you could begin by talking first about the bulb itself, as shown on the left-hand side of Figure 46, and then the socket, as shown on the right-hand side. The students are thus introduced to key items of vocabulary.

The two cutouts are then put together, as shown in Figure 47, and your description of the principles involved related to the

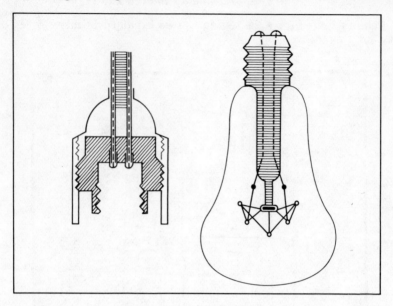

Figure 46

complete diagram. You must decide whether you want to include the vocabulary on the cutouts or superimpose it (as shown in Figure 47) by means of additional cards.

On the whole, however, this kind of presentation can be more effectively done by means of overlays on the overhead projector, which also allows you to present a larger image of the object to the class.

3.4 THE MAGNETBOARD AS AN AID TO ELICITING A TEXT

The same materials described in 3.3, or similar ones, could be used to elicit a text from the class: that is, to get the students to make up their own dialogues or stories relating to a scene displayed or built up on the magnetboard. For example, using the map in 3.3, the

Figure 47

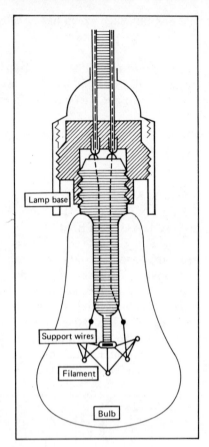

students themselves can be asked to suggest, in response to your questions or other cues, what Peter said when he answered the phone, what John said, what directions Peter gave John, and so on. Depending on your teaching aims, this could be either the initial activity or extension work derived from a previous activity. Similarly the map may be used to get the class to relate in narrative form what John did from the time he arrived at the station until he reached Peter's house. This is clearly very suitable as a follow-up activity for the dialogue presented in 3.3 because it involves using and adapting language which has already been presented. Part of the text might run as follows:

... and Peter told John how to get to his house. John came out of the station, turned left and went up the High Street past the car park, until he reached the bank on the corner. Then he ... (etc.)

Further suggestions for eliciting a text with the aid of the magnetboard are given in the section on oral composition (3.9).

3.5   THE MAGNETBOARD AS AN AID TO PRESENTING AND PRACTISING LANGUAGE ITEMS

This section shows you how you can use the magnetboard to present and practise a wide range of language items, focusing either on language structure (prepositions, tenses, passive forms, etc.) or on language functions (suggestions, advice, wishes, etc.). The list is intended only to be illustrative but it should be clear from it that the magnetboard has great potential for this purpose, particularly since the flexibility of the material allows situations used for presentation to be restructured for guided practice.

Figure 48

The magnetboard, like many other visual aids, is often regarded as being useful primarily for language teaching at an elementary level. As with other aids, however, its potential depends on how you use it. The scene in Figure 48, for example, could be exploited to present and practise the following structures:

(a) *past continuous tense forms* e.g. What was happening when Mrs Brown went into the room? (John) was watching TV. (Mary) was crying (etc.).
(b) *verb pattern: verb (see, etc.) + object + -ing form* e.g. What did Mrs Brown (see) when she went into the room? She saw (John) watching TV. She heard (Mary) crying (etc.).
(c) *conditional: if + past perfect/would have + past participle (see, etc.) + object + -ing form* e.g. What would Mrs Brown have (seen) if she had gone into the room? She would have seen (John) watching TV. She would have heard (Mary) crying (etc.).

The scene can then be restructured for related guided practice (Figure 49).

Figure 49

3.5.1 PREPOSITIONS AND PREPOSITIONAL PHRASES

English employs a wide range of prepositional forms which can only be mastered over a long period of time. Although it is not suggested that the magnetboard should always be used for teaching new prepositional uses, the advantages it has, deriving from the flexible nature of the material, should be kept in mind. These are illustrated below.

(a)   Objects can be moved around, placed in front of and behind one another (etc.), to illustrate *behind/in front of/on top of/ underneath* (etc.); see Figure 50.
Remember that unusual positions can be memorable! (See Figure 13.)

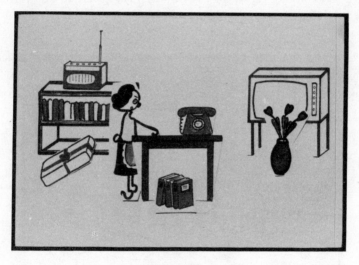

Figure 50

(b)   Objects can be moved across the board to show motion. The scene in Figure 51 can be used to demonstrate: *He ran after the bus. She fell under a car* (etc.).

Figure 51

(c) You can also illustrate spatial relationships such as *half in front of the* (*bookcase*) *and half in front of the* (*TV set*), *halfway between . . ., about* (*a metre*) *to the* (*left*) *of . . .* (etc.). See Figure 52.

Figure 52

3.5.2 TENSE FORMS

(a) The use of the magnetboard to demonstrate present time reference should be readily apparent. The scene in Figure 51 can also be used as a context for: *The boy is running after the bus. There is a car in front of the grocer's.* You can introduce the present perfect tense through actions which you have just performed. For example: *I've put the bookcase under the window. I've taken the vase of flowers off the bookcase and put it on the TV set* (etc.).

With the scene in Figure 53, a modified version of the one in 3.5, you can present and practise the use of the present perfect and the present perfect continuous tenses with *for* and *since*. The large clock shows the time now; the smaller clocks above each figure indicate when the action started. This provides a framework for: *How long has Mrs Brown been at the door? She's been there for five minutes. How long has John been watching TV? He's been watching it since 1.30* (etc.).

Figure 53

(b) The use of the magnetboard to provide a realistic context for practising past time reference has already been mentioned (see 2.5.3). If you start with the scene in Figure 54 and then re-structure it to create the one in Figure 55, you can present and practise structures like: *The bottle was on the table. Now it's near the armchair. There was a bottle on the table. Mrs Brown took the bottle off the table and put it near the arm-chair. The bottle that was on the table is now near the armchair.*

Figure 54

Figure 55

3.5.3   MODAL FORMS

(a)   *can/cannot* (for possibility) The scene in Figure 56 can be used to teach: (*Mr Smith*) *can see the girl on the donkey, but* (*he*) *can't see the bus in the road* (etc.).

Figure 56

(b)   *may/might* (for probability) The scene in Figure 57 can be used to practise: *The telephone may fall off the armchair. Someone may steal the handbag on the table. Somebody might fall over that vase of flowers!*

(c)   *going to* Either you or students taking your place can decide in which rooms to place the furniture (Figure 58) and say: *I'm going to* (*put the bookcase in the small room upstairs*) (etc.).

(d)   *used to* If you present the street scene first with one set of shop windows (bookshop, greengrocer's, baker's) and then move them around or use different ones, you can present:

This shop used to be a bookshop. Now it's a baker's (etc.).
Or: *There used to be a greengrocer's here. Now there's a café*
(etc.). Similarly with the room scene: *The TV set used to be in
the corner. There used to be a picture on that wall.* And with
the 'general exterior' scene: *This house used to be a club.
There used to be a swimming pool on the left over there* (etc.).

Figure 57

Figure 58

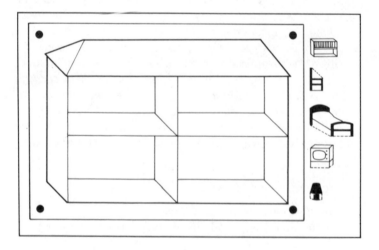

3.5.4 PASSIVE FORMS

One possible context for practising passive forms has already been suggested in the last paragraph of 3.2.1. You can also use the 'general exterior' scene with appropriate cutouts to present and practise: *The house is going to be turned into a* (*club*). *Those trees are going to be cut down. A new swimming pool is going to be installed* (etc.).

If you first show the room scene with furniture and other objects in disorder and then arrange things in the room (with the help of the students), you can practise: *Everything in the room has been arranged! The table's been put in the centre of the room. The armchair's been put in the corner. The pictures have been hung up. . . . and that old rug has been thrown away!*

3.5.5 CLAUSE TYPES

(a) *conditional type: if + simple present, will/may* See the room scene in Figure 57. You may use this to teach: *If you leave your handbag on the table, somebody may steal it. If you leave the vase of flowers on the floor, somebody will fall over them* (etc.).

(b) *while + past continuous, simple past* See the room scene in Figure 48. You may use this to practise: *While John was watching TV, Peter rode his bicycle round the room* (etc.).

(c) *after + past perfect, simple past* Using the street scene in Figure 51 with appropriate cutouts, you may present and practise: *Mrs Brown went to the baker's. After she'd been to the baker's, she went to the greengrocer's. As she came out of the greengrocer's she met a friend. After she'd talked to her friend for a while, she went across the road to . . .* (etc.). The cutout of Mrs Brown should be moved around as suggested in 3.5.1(b).

3.5.6 REPORTED STRUCTURES

(a) *Reported statements and questions*
Using the room scene in Figure 59, begin with exchanges like:

Mr Brown:	Have you seen my briefcase?
Mrs Brown:	Yes, it's behind your armchair.
Mr Brown:	And what have you done with my umbrella?
Mrs Brown:	I've put it near your briefcase.

Figure 59

These exchanges can then be transformed into their reported forms. *Mr Brown asked his wife whether she had seen his briefcase. She told him it was behind his armchair. He also asked what she had done with his umbrella. She said she had put it near his briefcase.*

(b) *Reported commands*
The section view of the house in Figure 58 can be used as a context for practising reported commands. Place all the furniture outside the house, together with cutouts of a man, a woman and two men (= furniture movers). As in (a) above, you should start with direct statements (e.g. *Mrs Brown to both men: Take the cupboard and put it in the large bedroom*) and move to reported commands (*Mrs Brown told the two men to take the cupboard and put it in the large bedroom*).

3.5.7   IDENTIFYING PEOPLE AND THINGS

(a)   You may arrange a number of cutouts of objects on the magnetboard (with or without a backdrop), some of which are known to the class while others are new. The students have to find out the names of the new objects by asking: *What's that thing (to the left of) the (cup)? What's that thing called—it's green and round? What do you call that thing with the (round top)?* (etc.). New objects in the beach scene (see 3.5.9 below), such as the lighthouse, the steamer, can be similarly introduced. Likewise with people: e.g. seen in the street. *What's that woman (outside the baker's) called?*

(b)   One cutout may be placed behind another, so that it is not clear what the half-concealed object is. The students have to ask: *What's that thing (under the rug)?* etc.

3.5.8   ASKING FOR AND GIVING DIRECTIONS AND INSTRUCTIONS

(a)   As we have seen (in 3.3) the backdrop of the town plan is particularly useful for teaching asking for and giving directions because the cutouts of places (bank, restaurant, cinema, etc.) can be placed in different positions to give numerous opportunities for practising: *Where's the (museum)? How do I get to the (nearest car park)? Can you tell me the way to (the library)? Could you tell me how to get to (the university)* + appropriate responses.

(b)   The backdrop of the room can be used to practise asking for and giving instructions. For example: *Where shall I put (the bookcase)? Where do you want me to put (the vase of flowers)? Shall I put the lamp on the (TV set) or on the (table)?* The class can make various suggestions until they reach agreement. The house in Figure 58 can be similarly used.

3.5.9   SUGGESTIONS

You may use the beach scene in Figure 60 to practise, for example:

Figure 60

Let's (go for a swim). How about (walking as far as the lighthouse)? Why don't we (take that boat and go for a sail)? etc. The students may raise objections (*I don't want to. It's too far*) and make counter proposals (*I'd rather sit and sunbathe*). See 3.6 for guidance on how this type of activity can be done through microdialogues.

3.5.10 ADVICE

Offering advice may be practised within the context of the room scene in Figure 57. For example: *You'd better not (leave your handbag on the table). You shouldn't (leave that typewriter on the edge of the table). If I were you, I wouldn't (put that vase of flowers on the floor)*, etc. Also with the beach scene in Figure 60. For example: *Don't (lie in the sun too long). You'd better not (try to climb those cliffs)*, etc.

3.5.11   LIKES, DISLIKES AND PREFERENCES

(a)   For practice at an elementary level, cutouts (e.g. of food) may be placed on the magnetboard to practise: *I like (bananas). I don't like (cheese). I prefer (oranges to bananas).*

(b)   You may also use cutouts of objects to symbolise activities. For example: book = reading, football = playing football. The students can then practise: *I (like) (playing football)*, etc.

(c)   With the beach scene you can practise likes and dislikes with reference to activities shown in or implied by the picture. For example: *I don't like (sunbathing). I prefer (swimming)*, etc.

3.5.12   WISHES

(a)   Cutouts of objects such as a typewriter, football, tennis racquet, bicycle (etc.) may be displayed on the magnetboard to suggest a page in a gift catalogue. The students can then say: *I'd like (a bike for my birthday). I wish I had (a tennis racquet like that)*, etc.

(b)   With the beach scene the students can practise as in (a) above *I wish I had (a boat like that,* etc.) and also *I wish I could (go sailing), I wish I knew how (to swim)*, etc.

3.6   THE MAGNETBOARD AS A CONTEXT FOR MICRO-DIALOGUE PRACTICE

Micro-dialogues are a useful and effective technique for providing a conversational framework, of two or three exchanges, within which structural items and language functions can be practised and integrated. The magnetboard can be used to present the practice situation to the students, who then continue practising with individual cuecards. If the magnetboard is used for the second stage, the situation has to be restructured by rearranging the cutouts on the board. Examples are given below.

3.6.1 MAGNETBOARD PRESENTATION + CUECARDS FOR PRACTICE

Present the model dialogue to the class, eliciting responses from individual students. The situation in Figure 61 is based on the backdrop of the room; cutouts of furniture and other objects to be located are placed on either side of the magnetboard.

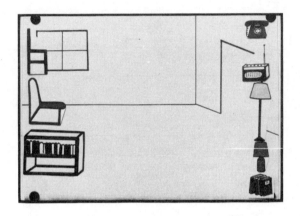

Figure 61

T: Where shall we put (the bookcase)?
S1: Oh, let's put it (under the window).
T: What do you think, . . .?
S2: Well, I'd rather put it (in the corner near the door).
T: All right. Let's put it there, then.

Invite one of the students to take your place and to choose the next object.

S1: Where shall we put (the armchair)?
S2: Oh, why not put it (near the bookcase).
S1: What do you think, . . .?
S3: No, let's put it (under the window).
S1: Well, I think I'll put it (near the bookcase).

Two similar but not identical models have now been presented. For further class practice at a more rapid pace, identify those students who have to provide further examples—it is important that they should know who they will be talking to and actually look at one another when they speak—and continue for as long as necessary. The students can then be given individual cuecards (Figure 62) and asked to practise on their own.

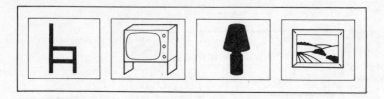

Figure 62

3.6.2 MAGNETBOARD PRESENTATION + RESTRUCTURED SCENE FOR FURTHER PRACTICE

(a) The first example illustrates structural practice at a fairly elementary level. The models, within the context of the scene in Figure 63, might be:

Figure 63

S1: I'm looking for (my handbag). Have you seen it?

S2: Yes, it's (on the table).

S1: Oh, that isn't mine. It's (Mary's).

Or:

S1: I'm looking for (John's umbrella). Have you seen it?

S2: Well, I think it's (behind the armchair).

S1: Oh, that isn't (his). It's mine.

The cutouts on the magnetboard are then placed in different positions and the students continue to practise in pairs.

(b) The second example illustrates practice with a function-focus at a more advanced level. See the magnetboard scene in Figure 57. Establish the models for practice. For example:

S1: You'd better not (leave your handbag on the table).

S2: Why (on earth) not?

S1: Well, someone might (steal) it.

S1: You shouldn't (leave that typewriter near the edge of the table), you know.

S2: Oh, why?

S1: Well, it might (fall off), of course.

S1: Oh, don't (put that vase of flowers on the floor).

S2: But why not?

S1: Well, someone's (bound to go and fall over them).

The cutouts on the magnetboard are then placed in different positions or replaced with different cutouts and the students continue to practise in pairs.

3.7 THE MAGNETBOARD AS A CONTEXT FOR GROUP ACTIVITIES

The magnetboard has no special potential for group work, but since the material is flexible, it is possible to use the material for activities like the following:

(a) The class is shown a room scene with the furniture and other objects arranged in a certain way. (Some features could be deliberately unacceptable: for example, the TV set is in front of the bookcase.) The students are then divided into groups to decide how they would like to arrange the furniture (they may draw a sketch map). When they have finished, the groups compare their decisions.

(b) The class is shown the backdrop of the room (or the house). A large selection of cutouts is displayed on either side of the magnetboard. The groups are then asked to decide which (fifteen) items they would use and where they would put them. Again, decisions (and reasons for decisions) are compared as in (a).

Similarly you may use the town plan to involve the students in developing their own town (using either of the procedures suggested in (a) and (b) above) and the street scene to get them to decide which shops they would like to have in the street and where they would place them.

3.8 THE MAGNETBOARD AS A CONTEXT FOR LANGUAGE GAMES

The games described in this section have been chosen because they are particularly effective with the use of magnetboard materials.

S2: I went to the supermarket and I bought (a pound of apples and a packet of tea) (etc.).

Notice that you can get the students to use a variety of patterns: *Will you go into town and buy me ...?/When you go to town, will you please buy me ...? If you go into town, would you mind buying me ...? If I go to town, I'm going to buy ...* (etc.).

The cutouts can also be varied to practise (for example) *For my birthday, I'd like ...* (with cutouts of items suitable as presents). *When I go to the beach, I always take ... When I went on holiday, I took in my suitcase ...*

(b) You may also use scenes built up on the magnetboard. For example, using the street scene, the key sentence may be: *While I was walking down the street, I saw (a fat woman crossing the road)* (etc.). Similarly with the beach scene: *While I was sitting on the beach, I watched (a man taking a photo)* (etc.).

3.9 THE MAGNETBOARD AS AN AID TO ORAL COMPOSITION

Oral composition may be an end in itself or a preparation for written work.

3.9.1

You may use the magnetboard to display picture composition charts. You may show these one at a time in sequence, as illustrated in Figure 64, focusing attention on each picture in turn and inviting the students to speculate about what happens next. You may also use the magnetboard to show only part of the sequence, as shown in Figure 65, so that the students have to guess what happened next or how the two pictures are related.

Figure 64

Figure 65

3.9.2

You may also build up a scene on the magnetboard for oral practice leading to oral composition. For example, with the scene in Figure 66, you may begin as follows: *The other morning, PC Smith went*

Figure 66

to the park . . . Then ask questions: *Who did he see at the entrance to the park? What did he say to the woman? What did he tell her to do?* Next, ask the students to produce a narrative based on this. For example: *The other morning, PC Smith went to the park. There he saw a woman waiting at the entrance in her car, so he told her she could not park there.* Then add the next cutout or cutouts (Figure 67) and continue. *Then he went into the park* (remember that the cutout of the policeman can be moved to elicit this). Again ask questions: *What did he see? What did he say to the boy?* and elicit the narrative: *Then he went into the park, where he saw a boy riding his bike on the grass. He told him not to do this.*

You may continue the oral composition by adding new cutouts to show what happened after this or you may ask the students to do this in writing. If you complete the story orally, you may either put different cutouts on the board as cues for the written version, so that it is not a replica of the oral preparation stage, or ask the students to write a composition from a different angle. For example, a simple variation would be: 'Re-tell the story from the point of view of PC Smith.' A more difficult version would be to ask the students to write the story in the form of a report.

Figure 67

3.9.3   USING DIAGRAMMATIC MATERIAL

The backdrop of the town, used in 3.2.2 as a context for a listening comprehension activity, may also be used for oral composition or as oral preparation for a writing activity. For the latter, oral work is developed around the version of the town as it appears in 3.2.2. The students are asked, for example: *How many areas is the town divided up into? Where are these areas?* Then each area is examined. For example: *What does the residential area consist of? What can you find on the housing estate? How many different types of houses are there? What are they? What facilities are there in the park?* The answers to some of these questions are 'open-ended': that is to say, the class may suggest a number of facilities for the park and different kinds of light industry to be found on the industrial estate.

After this oral preparation stage, the cutouts representing

various areas of the town are moved to new positions, as shown in Figure 68. This is the version of the town which they are asked to describe in writing, utilising the key language items which they have practised orally.

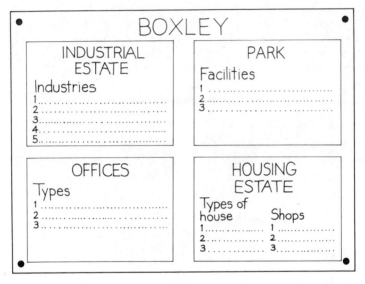

Figure 68

3.10 THE MAGNETBOARD AS AN AID TO TEACHING VOCABULARY

It should be clear from the discussion of techniques and procedures in 3.1 to 3.9 that vocabulary items can and should normally be presented and practised within the context of the activities described. To a large extent this can be done incidentally. An exception is the teaching of technical vocabulary (see 3.3.1), which in any case is likely to present the students with a heavier learning load.

The flexibility of the magnetboard allows new vocabulary to be introduced gradually and systematically, because you have complete control of the material (unlike a wall picture, for example, where items are visible whether or not you want them and therefore can be distracting). You can also decide how often and in what contexts to re-introduce particular items of vocabulary.

You can use magnetboard cutouts to ensure that the students understand differences of meaning between items in a lexical set. Figure 69 shows four different kinds of 'bag'. Wherever possible, you should include more than one example of an item, so that the students do not associate the word with a single image.

Figure 69

Remember that the students should always be encouraged to ask, when a cutout of a new vocabulary item is introduced: *What's that called?* or *What do you call the thing you have just (put near the bookcase)?*

3.11 THE MAGNETBOARD AS AN AID TO TEACHING READING

The magnetboard is a useful device for displaying and

manipulating material for promoting reading ability in the early stages.

3.11.1 WORD AND SENTENCE MATCHING

You may do this with words. For example, see Figure 70. The students may also be asked to match several items with the appropriate word card (Figure 71). If you are using the 'whole

Figure 70

Figure 71

sentence' approach, the students can be asked to match the complete sentence with the appropriate picture (Figure 72).

Figure 72

3.11.2   READING PRACTICE WITHOUT VISUAL CUES

You can also use word and sentence cards without any visual accompaniment (Figure 73). The word cards can be quickly manipulated to form new sentences (Figure 74).

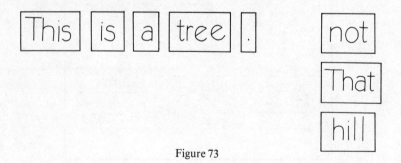

Figure 73

Figure 74

3.12 THE MAGNETBOARD AS AN AID TO TEACHING GRAMMAR

Here we are concerned with the use of materials which will help to explain or make more explicit word or sentence structure. A few examples are given in Figures 75-78.

3.12.1 WORD FORMATION

For example, the use of the suffix *-er* to form agent-type nouns from verbs (Figure 75).

Figure 75

3.12.2 WORD ORDER

For example, the difference in word order between affirmative and interrogative sentences (Figure 76).

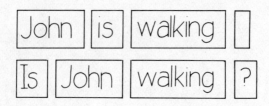

Figure 76

3.12.3   PHRASE STRUCTURE

For example, in combination with visuals, types of post-modifier in the noun phrase (Figure 77).

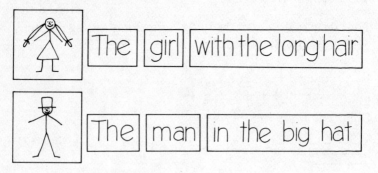

Figure 77

3.12.4   VOICE

For example, the deletion of the agent in passive constructions (Figure 78).

Somebody stole the book

The book was stolen

Figure 78

3.13 THE MAGNETBOARD AS AN AID TO TESTING

The flexibility of magnetboard materials makes it possible to use them as a framework for informal testing, especially of oral ability. Most of the situations described in the preceding sections can be adapted for testing purposes. For example, using a magnetboard scene like the one in Figure 79, you can make a number of true/false statements about it and ask the students to decide which ones are true and which are false.

Figure 79

The same scene or a similar one can be used to get the students to produce sentences or series of sentences, orally or in writing. These may be modelled on examples provided by you or, for practice in free expression, composed by the students themselves.

3.14   THE MAGNETBOARD AS AN AID TO PRESENTING INFORMATION

The general use of the magnetboard, as a device for displaying visual material such as wall charts, photos, magazine cutouts, was noted in 2.1.1. In addition, it can be used to display maps, charts and diagrams with a higher information content. The purpose of this may be mainly to provide background information. The advantage of using a magnetboard for this purpose is that you can build up the map or chart step by step. For example, with a map of a country, you can add the major cities, rivers and mountains one by one, together with any other information you want to provide (for example, about industries). You can also exploit other material

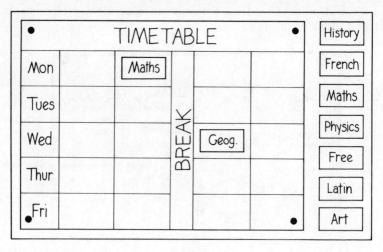

Figure 80

displayed in this way, such as calendars, timetables and agenda sheets, for language practice. The advantage of having, for example, a backdrop of a timetable like the one in Figure 80, together with appropriate cutouts, is that it is flexible: you can present it to the class already made up for one type of language activity, build it up with the help of their suggestions for another, and use different cutouts for yet another one. A backdrop of an agenda sheet or the page of a diary has a similar potential (Figure 81).

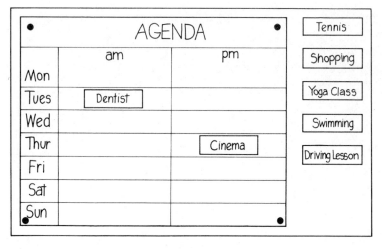

Figure 81

4 *Summing Up and Evaluation*

It should be apparent that, if you use the magnetboard along the lines suggested in Chapter 3 in combination with the kind of materials described in Chapter 2, the potential of this relatively simple visual aid for language teaching is very great indeed. Its relative neglect in many classrooms is probably due largely to the fact that its flexibility is not fully appreciated and very little use is made of different kinds of backdrops.

It has, of course, a special appeal to younger learners: in particular, they enjoy the activities that result from manipulating the material. They can also be asked to make their own material for use on the magnetboard. On the other hand, its effectiveness at different levels of language learning and its appeal to different types of student will depend largely on the kind of materials used and on the kind of activity it is used for. In general, perhaps, it should be used more selectively with adolescent and adult students.

In any case, before you decide to use it for a particular activity, you must always weigh up its advantages and disadvantages in comparison with other available aids. Is the blackboard quicker and equally effective? Would a particular set of materials be easier to handle in the form of transparencies on the overhead projector? Would a wall picture be more visually convincing? Of course, once you have invested either money in acquiring materials or time in making them, you will want to get the maximum return on your investment. But you should never over-use them: if you do, the learners themselves may reject the materials—and with them the activities they are being used for.

Appendix: *Sources of Materials*

1 MAGNETBOARDS

These are available from most stockists of educational aids (see the list below). Magnetboards are also sold for commercial purposes (e.g. for use in offices).

Suitable metal (zinc or tinplate) for making a magnetboard is usually available in ironmongers. The sources of supply vary, however, from country to country and in some countries it may be easier to find the right material in workshops.

2 MAGNETS (COUNTERS AND MAGNETIC STRIP)

These are also available from stockists of educational aids. Magnetic strip is also sometimes sold in large stores as 'handy' material for use in the home.

If you work in a school, you can get magnets made for you in the physics laboratory.

3 CUTOUTS

A set of cutouts for language teaching in package form, entitled *Materials for Language Teaching 3*, has been produced by Modern English Publications Ltd. This may be ordered through bookshops which sell EFL materials or obtained direct from Modern English Publications Ltd, Distribution Department, 8 Hainton Avenue, Grimsby (England).

STOCKISTS OF EDUCATIONAL MATERIALS

ADVA Services Ltd, 52 Poland Street, London W1V 3DF.
Educational Supply Association, Pinnacles, Harlow, Essex.
Visual Aid Centre, Websters Bookshops Ltd, 78 High Holborn, London WC1V 6NB.